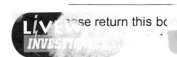 
Kickboxing

Kathy Galashan

Published in association with The Basic Skills Agency

Hodder & Stoughton

A MEMBER OF THE HODDER HEADLINE

Acknowledgements
Cover: Raoul Minsart
Photos: p 2 © Jerome Prevost; TempSport/Corbis; p 5 © Paul A. Souders/Corbis; p 8 © Ryan McVay/Photodisc; p 11 © Duomo/Corbis; p 17 © Action Plus; p 19 © Franck Sequin; TempSport/Corbis; p 22 © Mitchell Gerber/Corbis.

Every effort has been made to trace copyright holders of material reproduced in this book. Any rights not acknowledged will be acknowledged in subsequent printings if notice is given to the publisher.

The author would like to thank Sophie Pittaway and Bill Judd from K.O. Gym, London.

Orders: please contact Bookpoint Ltd, 39 Milton Park, Abingdon, Oxon OX14 4TD. Telephone (44) 01235 827720, Fax: (44) 01235 400454. Lines are open from 9.00–6.00, Monday to Saturday, with a 24-hour message answering service. Email address: orders@bookpoint.co.uk

British Library Cataloguing in Publication Data
A catalogue record for this title is available from the British Library

ISBN 0 340 80066 6

First published 2001
Impression number   10 9 8 7 6 5 4 3 2 1
Year   2007 2006 2005 2004 2003 2002 2001

Typeset by SX Composing DTP, Rayleigh, Essex.
Printed in Great Britain for Hodder & Stoughton Educational, a division of Hodder Headline Plc, 338 Euston Road, London NW1 3BH by Redwood Books Ltd, Trowbridge, Wilts.

Contents

Do you want to get fit?
Do you want to defend yourself?
Do you want to learn to fight?
Do you want to push yourself hard?

Then kickboxing is for you.

You get fit, really fit.
You learn to defend yourself.
It helps you learn control.
You have fun
and you feel good about yourself.
It gives you a real buzz of energy.

Thai boxing is now an Olympic sport.

1 What is Kickboxing?

Kickboxing is a martial art.
Martial art means 'art of war'.
It puts together the skills
of boxing and kicking.

Some people do kickboxing
for fitness.
For others it is a competitive sport.
It is a full-contact sport.
That means you can use
all your power.
You can aim
at all parts of the body.

It is fast.
It is flowing.
It can be dangerous.

2   When did Kickboxing Start?

Kickboxing comes from Thai boxing.
Thai boxing started in Siam in the 1600s.
It was started by warriors.
They wanted to practise
hand-to-hand fighting in peace time.
They used their whole body
to attack and defend.

They used to wrap
their hands in bandages
and dip them in broken glass.
This made a punch very dangerous.
Then they used boxing gloves.
It became a sport in a ring.

This kickboxer is preparing for his match.

Thai boxing uses punches,
elbows, knees and kicks.

Boxing and kickboxing
come from Thai boxing.
Kickboxing uses
the punches and kicks.
Boxing uses the punches
but not the kicks.

In the 1970s kickboxing became popular.
Rules were set up
and the sport was made safer.

Now Thai boxing is
a part of the Asian Olympic Games.
Maybe kickboxing will become
an Olympic sport soon.

3   Getting Started

The first thing
is to find a class.
The World Kickboxing Association
has a list of all clubs.
Try your local sports centre
or ask at a library.

Check that the teacher is registered.
Insurance is important too.
Then you are covered
if you get hurt.
A good teacher makes the class safe
and has insurance as well.

You don't need special clothes
to start with.
People wear tops
and shorts or loose trousers.
Clothes need to be comfortable.

Joining a class is the best way to learn kickboxing.

If you join a club
you can buy their kit.
Each club has their own kit.

You will need wraps
to protect your hands
and boxing gloves.
You will need shin pads
to protect against kicks.
Gum shields protect your teeth.
But you don't need
all that to start.

Just find a class and go along.

4   A Kickboxing Fitness Class

Anyone can join a kickboxing class.
You start with your level of fitness.
Then you get better.
A class is about working hard
and getting better.
It is not about being the best.

First there are warm-ups to music.
Techno music with a heavy beat
is a popular choice.
This type of music keeps the class moving.
It keeps it fast.

Then you practise punches and kicks.
You do it on your own to start with.
This is called shadow work.
It is hard work, very fast
but very exciting.

Use a puchbag to practise your kicks on.

Every class works with pads.
One person holds the pads
and the other punches and kicks.
The pads let you hit very hard
and build up your strength.
It feels good hitting and kicking
as hard as you can.

Sparring is working in twos.
This is a chance to practise moves
and to learn to defend yourself.
Blocking punches and kicks
is important.
So is getting out of the way.

You have to work
with your partner.
There are three rules
to working in pairs.

1.   Motivate.
       Help each other
       do the best you can.

2.   Correct each other.
       Tell each other
       what feels good and bad.

3.   Keep it safe.

In a large class you help each other.
A teacher can't be everywhere
all the time.

A class pushes you hard
so you become stronger.
You learn to keep going.
It helps to build up your endurance.
Your body learns to move
in new ways.
It becomes more flexible.
Muscles stretch
and joints become looser.

5 Gradings

Gradings are tests.
You move up the gradings
until you get a black belt.

A grading lasts about an hour.
It tests your fitness.
You do press-ups, sit-ups
and stretches.

You will be tested on how good
you are at punches and kicks.

Your instructor will need to see
your work on pads.
Padwork shows your power.

A grading tests sparring.
This shows your control
and your timing.
It shows if you can
attack and defend.

Then there is a part on the history
and background of kickboxing.
You also need to know
about first-aid
and how the body works.

Gradings push you to get better.
It feels good to pass.

6   Training

If you join a club
you can enter competitions.
But first comes the training.
Fighters build up power
with punch bags and medicine balls.
Long punch bags let you
practise kicking and punching.
Trainers drop heavy balls
on your stomach.
This makes the muscles strong.

Kicks and punches are practised
with a partner and on your own.
They are practised
over and over again.

Training makes the moves
part of you.
In a fight
there is no time to think
how to do a move.
Tactics are important
then your reflexes take over.

You need to train hard if you want to enter competitions.

7   Competitions

There are amateur and professional
competitions.
They take place in a boxing ring.

A kickboxing competition is
like a boxing match.
Competitors start in their corner
with a coach.
There is a referee and judges.

In an amateur competition
there are three rounds.
Points are given for punches and kicks
that hit the other person.

In a professional fight
there are twelve rounds.
You can win by points
or by a knockout.
You win a knockout if
the other person is on the floor
to a count of ten.

A professional kickboxing fight is very exciting.

A big professional fight is very exciting.
In Japan up to 50,000 people
watch a big fight.
There are TV cameras and big screens
to follow what goes on.
The crowd roars and shouts.
The kickboxers spin and dive
around the ring
throwing kicks and punches.
They move very fast
and a blow can mean a knockout.
They keep moving.
Remember a blow can hit
any part of the body.
The danger can come from
hands, arms, feet or legs.
Kickboxers need a cool head
and very quick reflexes.

Professionals get good money, too.
Top fighters can earn £100,000 a fight.

8   What People Say About Kickboxing

Mary

I go to a kickboxing fitness class.
I didn't like sport at school
but this is fun.
I'll never be good enough
for competitions
but that is not important to me.
I'm much fitter
than I was before.
The teacher is great.
As long as I work hard
she gives me lots of support.

Mohammed

I work in films.
I love Jackie Chan.
He's the best kickboxer ever.
His films are so exciting.
He moves brilliantly.

I want to be a stuntman.
Kickboxing is very useful.
It's great for fitness
and there is often kickboxing
in films and adverts.
It makes me think quickly too.

Jackie Chan's and Michelle Yeah's kickboxing skills have brought them success in many films.

Jo	I did a lot of boxing
	but this is better.
	It feels safer
	because I don't get hit
	on the head so much.
	I was a junior champion
	and I want to become
	a professional kickboxer.
	The money can be very good
	and it is a chance to travel.
	I train and run every day.
	The club is brilliant.
	There are people to help me
	and train with.
Sam	I've just started.
	The best thing is
	I learned kicks and punches
	in the very first class.
	I felt I was kickboxing straight away.

Rita

When life is difficult
a class makes me feel better.
I forget all the bad things.
A work-out with punching
and kicking
helps me feel on top again.
Also the people are great.
I've made all sorts of new friends.

Adam

I love sparring.
I like being better
than someone else.
It's a real kick to win,
to know my skill and my training
makes me a winner.

9   Finding Out More

The World Kickboxing Association

This has a good website.
You can get a list of clubs
and kickboxing events
and a whole lot more.
www.wka.co.uk

Cobra 2000
Martial Arts Equipment
115b Malden Road
London NW5
Tel. 020 72677894

A bookshop with magazines and information.
It has a catalogue and mail order.

Combat kickboxing magazine.

Try looking on the internet for kickboxing
associations like:
http://www.kickboxing.com

Glossary

amateur	someone who does something for pleasure
endurance	being able to keep going
flexible	being able to move well
gradings	a series of tests
judge	someone who decides how good a person is
kickboxing	a martial art
knockout	this is when you can't get up after a hit
martial art	art of war – martial arts cover the fighting sports that come from the East
medicine ball	a round ball of different weights
professional	someone who is paid for what they do
a punch bag	a heavy bag that takes a punch or kick
referee	someone who checks the rules are kept
reflexes	being able to act without thinking
registered	on a list of a professional organisation

shadow work	practising moves on your own
sparring	practising with another person
stuntman	someone who does dangerous acts in films or TV
Thai boxing	a martial art
warm-ups	exercises you do at the start of every class to stop you hurting yourself
warriors	soldiers